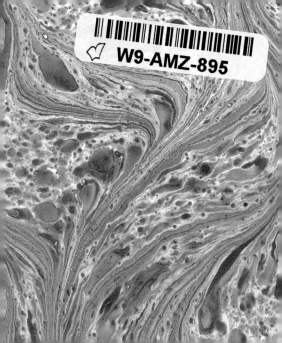

$\mathcal{T}$HIS BOOK BELONGS TO

_____

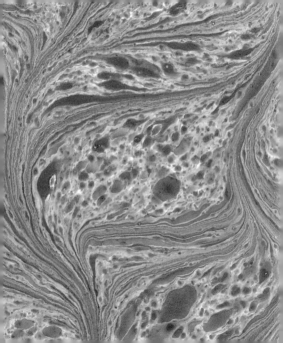

A LITTLE *Christmas* COOKBOOK

ARIEL BOOKS

ANDREWS AND McMEEL
KANSAS CITY

ISBN: 0-8362-3039-6

Library of Congress Catalog Card Number: 92-75640

Marbleized endpapers © 1993 by Katherine Radcliffe

A LITTLE CHRISTMAS COOKBOOK

Contents

PART 1
HORS D'OEUVRES

PART 2
MAIN COURSES

PART 3
SIDE DISHES

PART 4
DESSERTS, COOKIES, AND OTHER TREATS

INTRODUCTION

*C*hristmas is a time for remembrance: for reenacting traditions and for re-creating meals that we have known and loved since childhood. It is also the time for introducing— ever so gently— some new traditions that will, with time, become as cherished as any.

Christmas is also when we gather old and new friends to celebrate the season. In ancient times, the solstice was marked with a slow-burning yule log to commemorate the arrival of lengthening days. Now, we combine some of the pagan ritual with more modern celebrations, both secular and *religious. Choirs and carolers sing, hosts and hostesses plan parties, friends and family choose special gifts for one another, home cooks fill cookie jars to brimming, and children write wishful letters to Santa Claus.*

So often when we think of Christmas traditions, we hark back to England and, closer to home, New England. Both places conjure up images of frosty days; snowy woods; cold, starlit nights; and a home with cozy rooms warmed by a roaring fire. These rooms are decked with garlands of greenery, wreaths of holly, and a glittering Christmas tree. Children are bright-eyed with excitement; enticing aromas emanate from a big, warm kitchen; and, at least temporarily, all is right with the world.

ENGLISH CHRISTMAS

Christmas has been celebrated for centuries in England. As early as the 16th century, the holiday was a time for feasting and frolicking —although for a short time during the era of Oliver Cromwell, Christmas revelry was forbidden. During those bleak years, the Lord Mayor of London, on orders from Cromwell, had all festive greenery gathered and burned! But by the mid-1600s, Cromwell was gone, and the English immediately returned to marking the holidays.

Not until the days of Queen Victoria in the 1800s did Christmas in England take on the romance we today associate with it. During her long reign, Charles Dickens wrote his famed A CHRISTMAS CAROL, *and Tiny Tim, with the help of a reformed Ebenezer Scrooge, asked God to bless us, "every one."*

Victoria's German-born husband, Albert, introduced the Christmas tree to Buckingham Palace. Following the custom of his country, he set small trees on tables, surrounded them with gifts, and carefully lit candles placed on the branches. So delighted with the custom were his wife and children that the royal family embraced it wholeheartedly, and decorated evergreen trees soon became a fixture in all English homes at Christmastime.

AMERICAN CHRISTMAS

No one knows for certain when the first American decked a tree, but a reliable record exists describing how Charles Follen, a German refugee living in

Boston, trimmed and lighted a tree for his son as early as 1832. No doubt, Hessian soldiers introduced Americans to the idea even earlier, during the Revolution. And by the end of the 19th century, timber-rich and expansive America had replaced the small tabletop trees with the floor-to-ceiling extravaganzas we know today.

As well as decorating the Christmas tree, nearly every American household during the last century followed the custom of hanging a stocking for Santa to fill on Christmas Eve. Even today, tiny feet excitedly pad from bedroom to living room early on Christmas morning to admire what the jolly old elf has left.

Stockings are an outgrowth of the European custom of leaving shoes out for the Wise Men to fill with coins or trinkets. As early as 1809,

Washington Irving, the New York writer and historian, wrote of hanging a stocking by the chimney on "St. Nicholas eve," and accounts exist of President Andrew Jackson inviting his niece to hang a stocking at the White House in 1835. By the end of the century, enterprising businessmen were selling decorated bright red stockings—some already filled.

In the late 19th and early 20th centuries, it was customary to slip a whole orange into the toe of the stocking. Like many foods, fruit was scarce in the winter months, so the semitropical orange was a special treat. As the night progressed and the fire burned to embers, the fruit's fragrance filled the air, tickling youngsters awake with its pungent aroma.

CHRISTMAS FOOD

Christmas trees and stockings aside, it is the kitchen that, in so many households, is the heart of Christmas. This is where plans are made, meals begun, and parties ended. Throughout the joyous season, family members and friends, adults and children, wander in and out, sampling this and experimenting with that. But nothing surpasses the satisfaction of the cook who, beaming with pride, pulls a tray of cookies, a perfectly baked cake, or a plump golden turkey from the oven.

Beginning early each December, dedicated home cooks stock their cupboards with flour, sugar, spices, nuts, and chocolate and their refrigerators with eggs, butter, and cream. Day after day is devoted to baking, creating cookies, pies, and cakes that serve as special holiday treats for their families and as loving gifts for relatives, neighbors, teachers, and co-workers. Christmas baking is, for many, a treasured yearly ritual, shared again and again with children and grandchildren.

While English cooks faithfully prepare plum pudding, also called Christmas pudding, American cooks are more likely to make fruitcakes, butter cookies, and pies of all description.

But Christmas cooking involves far more than baking. The Christmas table is set with vegetables, breads, and cranberry sauces, as well as a magnificent roast turkey stuffed with savory dressing or roast beef accompanied by rich gravy. If we begin the meal with hors d'oeuvres, they generally are light and easy—no one wants to fill up before the main event.

The Christmas feast is a welcome and much loved one, culminating in a large, clamorous gathering of family and friends. Some, after sampling dish after dish, gratefully retire to the hearth to nap or talk quietly; others choose a brisk walk in the chilly afternoon air; while still others find themselves in the kitchen, cleaning up and reviewing the day filled so satisfactorily with a good meal, good conversation, and the company of those we love best.

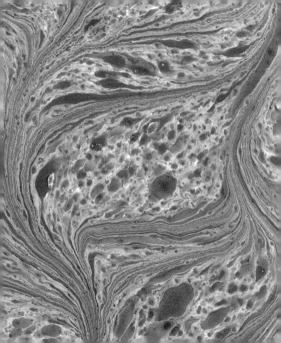

Part 1

HORS D'OEUVRES

BLUE CHEESE DIP WITH WINTER FRUIT

*T*raditionally, a good Stilton or other blue-veined cheese is served with ripe fruit after the meal. Here, we break with custom and serve it before as an easy full-flavored dip.

---

3 oz. blue cheese or Gorgonzola, crumbled
1/4 cup milk
1/2 cup plain yogurt
1 tbl. finely chopped scallions
1 tsp. fresh lemon juice
Dash of pepper
1 tsp. chopped scallions, for garnish

2 to 3 firm, ripe pears, sliced
2 to 3 tart apples, sliced
Large bunch green or red grapes

Stir the crumbled cheese and milk together in a bowl, mashing the cheese with the back of a spoon or fork.

Add the yogurt, 1 tbl. scallions, lemon juice, and pepper. Stir well. Cover and refrigerate until ready to serve.

To serve, spoon the dip into a small bowl and garnish with 1 tsp. scallions. Place on a large platter surrounded by sliced fruit and grapes. **Makes about 1 cup dip.**

HERBED CHEESE STICKS

Serve these cheese sticks with glasses of sherry.

---

1 sheet frozen puff pastry, thawed
1 large egg white, lightly beaten
1/4 cup grated Parmesan cheese
1/2 tsp. dried thyme
1/2 tsp. dried tarragon
1/2 tsp. dried rosemary
Dash of pepper

Preheat the oven to 375°F.

On a lightly floured surface, roll the thawed pastry into a 10″-by-15″ rectangle. Brush with egg white. Sprinkle with the cheese, herbs, and pepper. With your fingertips, press the cheese and herbs gently into the pastry.

Using a sharp knife, cut the pastry crosswise into 1″ strips. Twist each strip into a spiral and squeeze the ends tightly. Lay the strips on an ungreased baking sheet about 1″ apart. Bake for about 15 minutes until browned and crisp. Remove the twists from the baking sheet and cool on a wire rack. **Makes 15 sticks.**

SPICY CRABMEAT TOASTS

*C*rab, shrimp, and oysters are considered winter
delicacies that can make a Christmas feast even
more special.

---

18 to 20 1/2″ slices French bread, lightly toasted
6 to 6 1/2 oz. fresh or canned crabmeat, drained
1/2 cup mayonnaise
1 tsp. Dijon mustard
1 tsp. prepared horseradish
1/4 tsp. cayenne pepper
Dash of black pepper
3 to 4 tbl. grated Parmesan cheese

Preheat the broiler. Lay the bread slices on ungreased baking sheets about 1″ apart.

Stir the crabmeat, mayonnaise, mustard, horseradish, and cayenne and black peppers together in a bowl. Spoon equal amounts on top of each bread slice. Sprinkle each with Parmesan cheese.

Broil for about 5 minutes until the crabmeat mixture is hot and bubbling. Serve immediately. **Makes 18 to 20 toasts.**

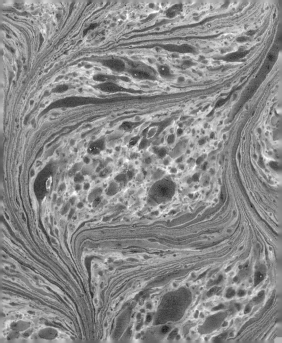

Part 2

MAIN COURSES

Holiday Roast Turkey with Old-Fashioned Apple Dressing

*After turkey was introduced in England
sometime during the 16th century, it was slow to
replace boar's head as a traditional Christmas
offering. Even today, it often is usurped by goose
in the British Isles. Americans tend to prefer
turkey. Either a turkey or a goose, roasted golden
and stuffed with redolent dressing, makes a
glorious centerpiece for the holiday feast.*

1/2 cup (1 stick) butter
1 1/2 cups chopped onion
6 oz. bulk pork sausage, crumbled
8 cups day-old bread cubes (10 to 12 slices)
1 1/2 cups peeled, cored, and diced tart apple
3/4 cup water or chicken broth
2 tbl. chopped parsley
1 tsp. dried sage
1 tsp. poultry seasoning
1 12- to 14-pound fresh turkey, giblets removed
Vegetable oil, for brushing

Melt the butter in a large skillet over medium heat. Add the onions and cook for about 5 minutes until softened. Add the sausage and cook for about 10 minutes until cooked through, stirring occasionally. Add the bread cubes, apple, water or broth, parsley, and seasonings and cook for 5 to 8 minutes, stirring gently. Cool the dressing slightly before stuffing the turkey, or, if you are not using it right away, cover and refrigerate it.

Preheat the oven to 325°F.

Rinse the turkey with cold water and drain well. After handling raw turkey, wash all work surfaces, utensils, and your hands with soapy warm water.

Stuff the neck and body cavities with the dressing. Pack the dressing quite firmly into the turkey but leave a little room for expansion. Spoon any leftover dressing into a buttered casserole, cover, and refrigerate.

Truss the turkey legs. Put the turkey, breast side up, on a rack set in a roasting pan. Insert a meat thermometer into the thigh but do not let it touch the bone. Brush the turkey with oil.

Roast the turkey, uncovered, for 4 to 4½ hours until the meat thermometer registers 180 to 185°F in the thigh. The drumsticks will feel loose, and their juices will run clear. About 50 minutes before the turkey is done, put the casserole with the dressing in the oven to heat.

Let the turkey stand for about 20 minutes before carving. **Serves 12 to 14.**

COUNTRY CORNBREAD STUFFING

*D*ressing turkey with a simple cornbread stuffing evokes a warm, bright farm kitchen— a comfortable refuge from the cold, snow-covered fields and country lanes.

3/4 cup (1 1/2 sticks) butter

2 cups chopped onion

1 cup chopped celery

1/2 cup chopped green bell pepper

1/2 cup chopped red bell pepper

1 clove garlic, chopped

8 oz. bulk pork sausage, crumbled

1 recipe day-old (slightly stale) Farmhouse
  Cornbread (pg. 48), crumbled

1 cup water or chicken broth
3 tbl. chopped parsley
2 tsp. dried sage

Melt the butter in a large skillet over medium heat. Add the onions, celery, bell peppers, and garlic. Cook gently for about 10 minutes until softened. Add the sausage and cook for about 10 minutes longer until cooked through, stirring occasionally. Add the cornbread, water or broth, parsley, and sage. Season to taste with salt and pepper. Cook over medium heat for about 10 minutes longer. Cool the dressing slightly before stuffing a turkey, or, if you're not using right away, cover and refrigerate it. **Makes about 6 cups stuffing, enough for a 12- to 14-pound turkey.**

ROAST BEEF WITH RICH PAN GRAVY

The English have enjoyed a good, juicy roast beef on the holiday table since the days of Queen Elizabeth I. Serve it with Yorkshire Pudding (pg. 50) for a merry yuletide feast.

Roast beef:
1 6- to 8-pound rolled, boneless rib roast
Salt and pepper

Gravy:
3 to 4 tbl. pan drippings
About 1 1/2 cups water or beef broth
1/4 cup all-purpose flour

Roast beef:

Preheat the oven to 325°F.

Place the roast on a rack set in a shallow roasting pan and season with salt and pepper. Insert a meat thermometer into the center of the roast.

Roast for 2¼ to 3 hours. For rare meat, the thermometer will register 140°F; for medium meat, 160°F; and for well-done meat, 170°F.

Gravy:

Remove the roast from the pan and put it on a serving platter. Pour the pan drippings into a large glass measuring cup. Skim off the fat and return 3 to 4 tbl. of fat to the roasting pan. Discard the remaining fat. (If you're making Yorkshire Pudding [pg. 50], set

aside ½ cup of the pan drippings in the measuring cup.)

Add enough water or broth to the pan drippings in the measuring cup to equal 2 cups of liquid. Set aside.

Add the flour to the roasting pan and stir the flour and fat together over low heat. Be sure to stir in any dark bits in the pan. When this mixture is bubbling, add the liquid. Stir and cook over medium heat until smooth and hot. Season with salt and pepper. Serve immediately with the roast beef. **Serves 12 to 16; makes about 2 cups gravy.**

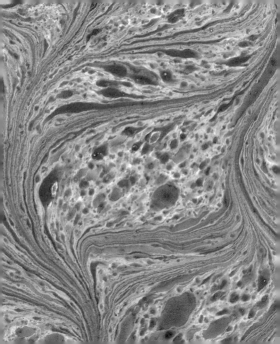

Part 3

SIDE DISHES

CHRISTMAS CRANBERRY SAUCE

*B*right red and cheerful, cranberry sauce is a must on the holiday table; in fact, serving turkey without it is like wrapping a present but forgetting the bow.

---

1 3/4 cups sugar
4 cups fresh cranberries
1 cup water
1 cup orange juice
1 tbl. coarsely grated orange zest
1 tbl. fresh lemon juice

Combine all the ingredients in a large saucepan and stir over high heat until boiling. Reduce the heat and simmer for 5 to 6 minutes until the berries pop open. Let the sauce cool before serving it or refrigerate it for 3 to 4 days. **Makes 4 to 5 cups sauce.**

STRING BEANS AMANDINE

Pan-browned almonds dress plain green beans in holiday finery.

---

2 tbl. butter
3 tbl. slivered almonds
2 10-oz. pkg. frozen French-style green beans,
　　cooked as package directs and kept hot
Salt and pepper
Fresh lemon juice

Melt the butter in a skillet over medium heat. Add the almonds; raise the heat a little; and cook, stirring occasionally, for 4 to 5 minutes until golden.

Toss the cooked almonds and butter with the cooked beans. Season to taste with salt and pepper and lemon juice. Serve immediately. **Serves 6 to 8.**

BAKED CANDIED SWEET POTATOES

Sweet potatoes are thought of as strictly American fare, although they turn up in the cooking of other lands as well. We cannot imagine Christmas dinner without this rich, buttery casserole— topped or not with marshmallows.

14 to 16 medium-sized sweet potatoes
3/4 cup packed light brown sugar
1/2 cup (1 stick) butter, cut up
1 tsp. salt
1 to 2 tsp. pepper
1/4 cup orange juice
1 tbl. finely grated orange zest
1 1/2 cups miniature marshmallows (optional)

Peel the sweet potatoes and cut them into large pieces. Put the potatoes in a large pot and add enough water to cover by 2" to 3". Bring the water to a boil. Lower the heat to medium-high and cook, uncovered, at a gentle boil for about 20 minutes until the potatoes are fork-tender. Drain and cool until you can handle the potato pieces.

Preheat the oven to 375°F.

Cut the potatoes into ½″-thick slices. Layer a third of the potato slices on the bottom of a 3-qt. casserole. Top with a third of the brown sugar and butter, a sprinkling of salt and pepper, a scant 1½ tbl. of the orange juice, and 1 tsp. of the orange zest. Repeat this procedure two more times with the remaining potato slices and other ingredients, except the marshmallows.

Bake the casserole, uncovered, for 45 to 50 minutes until the sugar melts and forms a glaze. Top the casserole with the marshmallows, if desired, and bake for 6 to 7 minutes longer until the marshmallows

are lightly browned. Serve immediately.
Serves 12 to 14.

Farmhouse Cornbread

Cornbread is as authentically American as a Grandma Moses painting. Serve it hot from the oven for Christmas breakfast or use it in the Country Cornbread Stuffing (pg. 32).

---

4 tbl. (1/2 stick) butter, melted
1 cup white or yellow cornmeal
1 cup all-purpose flour
2 tsp. baking powder
1/2 tsp. salt
1 cup milk
2 large eggs

Preheat the oven to 400°F. Grease an 8″-square pan with 1 tbl. of the melted butter.

Combine the cornmeal, flour, baking powder, and salt and whisk well. Add the milk, the remaining melted butter, and the eggs, whisking until well mixed. Pour the batter into the prepared pan. Bake for 20 to 25 minutes. **Serves 8 to 10; makes enough for 1 recipe Country Cornbread Stuffing.**

YORKSHIRE PUDDING

*Puffed and golden brown, freshly made
Yorkshire pudding crowns the Christmas table.*

---

4 eggs
2 cups milk
2 cups all-purpose flour
1 tsp. salt
1/2 cup pan drippings from Roast Beef with Rich
   Pan Gravy (pg. 34)

Preheat the oven to 450°F.

Whisk together the eggs and milk. Add the flour and salt and whisk until smooth.

Pour the pan drippings into a 17"-by-10" roasting pan or similarly sized shallow casserole. Heat the drippings in the oven for 3 to 4 minutes. Pour the batter into the hot pan and bake for about 15 minutes until puffy and golden brown. Serve immediately. **Serves 12 to 14.**

CRIMSON BEETS

Rich, earthy beets add a splash of festive color to the holiday table.

2 pounds fresh beets
3 tbl. butter
2 tbl. chopped onion
1 tbl. cornstarch
1/3 cup sugar
3/4 cup orange juice
1/4 cup cider vinegar
Salt and pepper

Wash and trim the beets. Put the beets in a large pot and add enough water to cover by

2" to 3". Bring the water to a boil. Lower the heat to medium-high and cook, uncovered, at a gentle boil for 40 to 45 minutes until the beets are fork-tender. Drain and cool until you can handle the beets. Slip off the skins. Chop the beets into cubes and set them aside.

Melt the butter in a skillet and saute the onions for 4 to 5 minutes until softened. Add the cornstarch, sugar, orange juice, and vinegar. Stir over medium heat for 3 to 4 minutes until the sauce is smooth and slightly thickened.

Add the beets and stir gently to coat with sauce. Cook over medium-low heat until the beets are heated through. Season to taste with salt and pepper. **Serves 6 to 8.**

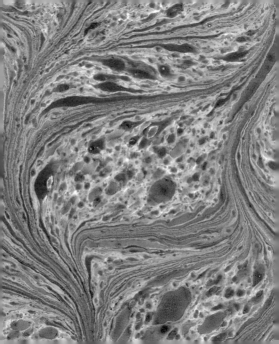

Part 4

DESSERTS,
COOKIES, AND
OTHER TREATS

YULETIDE MINCEMEAT PIE

*T*he ancestor of this Christmas pie is from Cumberland in Great Britain, where it was called a "sweet" or "standing" pie. Today, English and American cooks make mincemeat pie at Christmastime, as either individual tartlets or a large pie, such as this one. Nowadays, the pies don't always include meat.

Pie dough:
2 cups all-purpose flour
1 tsp. salt
6 tbl. (3/4 stick) chilled butter, cut up
6 tbl. chilled vegetable shortening, cut up
5 to 6 tbl. ice water

Mincemeat filling:

3 cups mincemeat (1 28-oz. jar)

1 cup chopped apple

1/2 cup chopped pear

1/4 cup chopped walnuts or pecans

1 tbl. finely grated orange zest

2 tsp. finely grated lemon zest

2 tbl. rum (optional)

1/4 tsp. freshly grated nutmeg

2 tbl. butter (optional)

Pie dough:

Mix the flour and salt and then add the butter and shortening. Use a knife or your fingertips to blend until the mixture resembles coarse crumbs.

Sprinkle the ice water a tablespoon at a time over the flour mixture, tossing until the dough just comes together. Gather the dough into a ball, wrap it in plastic, and refrigerate it for at least 1 hour or for up to 2 days.

Divide the dough into 2 pieces, one slightly larger than the other. Return the smaller piece to the refrigerator. On a lightly floured surface, roll the larger piece of dough into a 12″ circle. Lay the circle into a 9″ pie plate and trim any overhang.

Mincemeat filling:
Preheat the oven to 400°F.

Combine the mincemeat, apples, pears, nuts, and orange and lemon zest in a large bowl. Add the rum (if desired) and the nutmeg and toss to combine. Spoon the filling into the pie crust, mounding it slightly in the center. Dot with butter, if desired.

On a lightly floured surface, roll the smaller piece of dough into a 10″ circle. Lay the circle on top of the mincemeat filling, crimping the edges together with a fork. Cut 2 or 3 air vents in the top crust.

Bake for 30 to 35 minutes until bubbling and lightly browned. **Serves 8 to 10.**

HOLIDAY PECAN PIE

A rich nut pie, such as this pecan pie, is perfect on the Christmas table. Serve it with vanilla ice cream or whipped cream.

Pie dough:
1 1/4 cups all-purpose flour
1/2 tsp. salt
3 tbl. chilled butter, cut up
3 tbl. chilled vegetable shortening, cut up
2 to 3 tbl. ice water

Pecan filling:
3 tbl. packed dark brown sugar
2 tbl. all-purpose flour

3 eggs
1 1/2 cups dark corn syrup
1 cup pecan halves
1 tsp. vanilla extract
2 tbl. butter (optional)

Pie dough:
Mix the flour and salt and then add the butter and shortening. Use a knife or your fingertips to blend until the mixture resembles coarse crumbs.

Sprinkle the ice water a tablespoon at a time over the flour mixture, tossing until the dough just comes together. Gather the dough into a ball, wrap it in plastic, and refrigerate it for at least 1 hour or for up to 2 days.

On a lightly floured surface, roll the dough into a 12″ circle. Lay the circle into a 9″ pie plate and trim any overhang.

Pecan filling:
Preheat the oven to 350°F.

Combine the brown sugar and flour and toss well. Then stir in the eggs and whisk well. Add the corn syrup, pecan halves, and vanilla. Spoon the filling into the pie crust. Dot with butter, if desired.

Bake for 45 to 50 minutes until a knife inserted in the center comes out clean and the filling is slightly puffed and browned. **Serves 8 to 10.**

GRANDMA'S FRUITCAKE

*For centuries, cooks have made fruitcakes in
anticipation of the December holidays, usually
beginning their preparations early in the fall when
the nuts are ripe and dried fruits are readily
available at the market. Also called Christmas
cakes, these heady confections are served both
frosted and not and are expected tariff on the
Christmas afternoon tea table.*

---

3 cups all-purpose flour
2 tsp. baking powder
1 tsp. salt
1 tbl. ground cinnamon
1 tsp. ground nutmeg

1/2 tsp. ground allspice
2 cups chopped mixed candied fruits
2 cups raisins
1 cup golden raisins
1 1/4 cups chopped pitted dates
2 cups coarsely chopped walnuts
4 eggs
2 cups packed dark brown sugar
1 1/4 cups orange juice
3/4 cup (1 1/2 sticks) butter, melted and cooled
1/4 cup molasses
Rum or brandy (optional)

Prcheat the oven to 300°F. Grease two 9"-by-5" loaf pans and line them with waxed paper.

Whisk together the flour, baking powder, salt, and spices. Add the candied fruits, raisins, dates, and nuts and toss to coat them with the dry ingredients.

Beat the eggs with an electric mixer until light. Mix in the brown sugar, orange juice, melted butter, and molasses. Add this to the fruit mixture and stir well. Spoon the batter into the prepared pans to fill about halfway.

Bake for 2 hours or until a toothpick inserted in the centers comes out clean. Let the cakes cool in their pans set on wire racks.

When they're cool, turn out the cakes from the pans and peel off the waxed paper. Wrap them in foil or plastic to keep moist and refrigerate until serving. They keep for up to 1 month.

Alternatively, wrap the cooled cakes in cheesecloth saturated with rum or brandy. Wrap them tightly in foil and refrigerate. Change the cheesecloth, saturating it again, every week. The rum- or brandy-soaked fruit-cakes keep for 2 to 3 months. **Serves 25 to 30.**

CHRISTMAS SUGAR COOKIES

*C*hristmas without cookies is unheard of in most homes. These sugar cookies are ideal for shaping with an assortment of cutters and then decorating with tinted frosting.

Cookies:
2 1/4 cups all-purpose flour
1 tsp. baking powder
1/2 cup sugar
1/3 cup packed light brown sugar
3/4 cup (1 1/2 sticks) butter, softened
1 egg
1 tsp. vanilla extract

Decoration:
Colored sugar crystals and red hots (optional)

Frosting:
1/4 cup (1/2 stick) butter, softened
4 cups confectioners' sugar
1 tsp. vanilla extract
Pinch of salt
2 to 3 tbl. milk
Food coloring (optional)

Cookies:
Whisk together the flour and baking powder. Set aside.

Cream the sugars and butter with an electric mixer until light and fluffy. Add the egg and vanilla and beat well. Beat in the flour mixture until blended.

Shape the dough into 2 pieces and wrap each in waxed paper. Refrigerate them for at least 2 hours or overnight.

Preheat the oven to 350°F.

On a lightly floured surface, roll out one piece of dough about ¼" thick. Keep the remaining dough refrigerated.

Using cookie cutters, cut out cookies. Lay them on ungreased baking sheets about 1" apart. Gather the scraps and roll the dough again and cut out more cookies.

Decoration:
Decorate the cookies with colored sugar crystals and red hots, if desired.

Bake for 10 to 12 minutes until golden. Cool on wire racks. Repeat this procedure with the remaining half of dough.

Frosting:

Mash the butter with a fork until smooth. Add the confectioners' sugar, vanilla, and salt and whisk. Add enough milk for good spreading consistency.

If desired, divide the frosting into small bowls and add food coloring.

Spread the frosting on cooled cookies and decorate further with colored sugar crystals and red hots. **Makes 40 to 48 cookies.**

CANDIED APPLES

Caramel-covered apples were a special holiday treat in the days before large candy companies put commercial candy bars in every corner store. Even today, rosy-cheeked children, just in from sledding or skating, will delight in these sweet apples.

---

5 to 6 tart apples
5 to 6 thick Popsicle sticks or skewers
1 14-oz. pkg. caramels
3 tbl. water or milk

Wash and dry the apples and remove the stems. Insert the Popsicle sticks or skewers in the stem ends of the apples, making sure they are well lodged.

Combine the caramels and the water or milk in the top of a double boiler over simmering water. Stir occasionally with a wooden spoon until smooth and hot. Remove from heat.

Line a baking sheet with waxed paper. Grease the paper. Dip an apple into the caramel, turning it to coat completely. Let the excess drip back into the pan. Place the apple with the stick upright on the waxed paper. Repeat with the remaining apples and caramel. Chill the apples until set. **Makes 5 to 6 apples.**

HOT MULLED CIDER

Seventeenth-century country gentry discovered the joys of warm punch when rum was introduced to England from the West Indies. Hot mulled cider is a nonalcoholic substitute for the more potent punches of those times. Despite howling winds and icy roads, it will warm both traveler and host.

---

1 gallon fresh apple cider
4 cinnamon sticks
1 tbl. whole cloves
1 tbl. whole allspice
1 tsp. whole mace

Heat the cider in a large pot over high heat.

Wrap the cinnamon sticks, cloves, allspice, and mace in a double thickness of cheesecloth. Secure the bag with a piece of kitchen string. When the cider begins to boil, drop the cheesecloth bag into the pot, reduce the heat, and simmer for 8 to 10 minutes. Remove the bag and ladle the hot cider into mugs. **Serves 15 to 20.**

ELFIN EGGNOG

Eggnog—a rich, creamy indulgence reserved for Christmas and New Year's parties—has its roots in sweet syllabub, an old English favorite made with sugar syrup, milk, cream, and wine. A recipe for the nog allegedly served during George Washington's presidency calls for brandy, rye, rum, and sherry as well as a dozen eggs and a quart of heavy cream!

6 egg yolks

6 tbl. sugar

*5 cups milk or 4 1/2 cups milk and 1/2 cup
   brandy*

1 cup heavy cream

2 tbl. freshly grated nutmeg

Whisk the egg yolks and sugar together in a heavy saucepan. Add 2 cups of the milk. Cook the mixture over medium-low heat, whisking often, for 4 to 5 minutes until it bubbles and thickens enough to coat the back of a spoon or until it reaches 160°F. Maintain this temperature for 1 minute. (Watch the custard carefully, taking care it does not scorch.) Immediately remove the custard from the heat. Add the remaining milk and

stir well. Let the custard cool completely. If using brandy, stir the brandy into the custard after it cools.

Pour the cooled custard into a metal or glass container, cover, and refrigerate it for at least 2 hours.

Whip the cream to soft peaks with an electric mixer. Gently stir the whipped cream into the cold eggnog. Serve in cups with a sprinkling of nutmeg. **Serves 12 to 14.**

The text of this book was set in Caslon 540, the recipe titles in Caslon Openface, and the introduction and ingredient lists in Caslon 540 Italic by Dix Type Inc., of Syracuse, New York.

*Book design by
Diane Stevenson/Snap-Haus Graphics*

Illustrations by Victoria Lisi

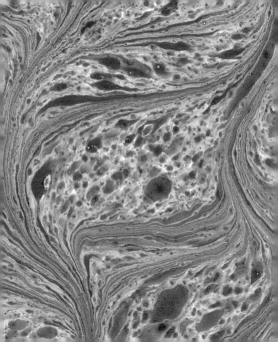